First Baptist
V E N I C E

312 West Miami Avenue
Venice, FL 34285
941.485.1314
fbcvenice.org

A Journey to Faithfulness

A 40 DAY DEVOTIONAL JOURNAL

By Heidi and Tim Guthrie

Published by

ESM Publishing

A Division of
Eklund Stewardship Ministries

A Journey to Faithfulness

A 40 DAY DEVOTIONAL JOURNAL

Copyright | Heidi and Tim Guthrie

ISBN: 978-1-60402-221-6

Design and Layout: The Ad Agency, Arlington, Texas

Printed in the United States of America

No More Footprints

If life is "Footprints in the Sand,"
Then faith, the imprint, cannot last,
And like the fool who built his house
You'll have no marker from the past.

A man who walks along the beach
May turn to see that God's been near,
But soon a storm will beat his shore
And the evidence will disappear.

It's in the hours of doubt and fear
That God shows up in ways unknown,
And we look back to see our pain
As pillars forged of toughest stone.

So build your faith upon the Rock
With monuments to mark each day,
That those on shore will see your God
In stones that time can't wash away.

- Heidi Guthrie

Introduction

We recently celebrated sixteen years of marriage with a trip to one of the highest points of Ski Mountain in the Smoky Mountains of Gatlinburg, Tennessee. We were packed and ready to go when we received a phone call that our visit would need to be delayed by at least a day due to an unexpected spring snow. We were disappointed, but who could have predicted four inches on the very romantic federal holiday of - you guessed it - Tax Day?

Once the weather cleared and the snow melted, we were given a hand-drawn map and the okay to travel up to our chalet. As we made our way up the mountain, we could easily see why we had been cautioned, and our disappointment soon turned to gratitude. The only path to our destination was fraught with hairpin turns, precarious one lane paths along a cliff's edge, and astonishing climbs in elevation. With our springtime mentality, we would not have been prepared for such a journey only hours before.

Perhaps you are there, or maybe your church is. It is your season of spring with exciting new growth, fresh beginnings, and hope for the future. You are heading up that mountain on a wonderful journey, but we have to ask... have you checked the weather? Are you adequately prepared for your journey? Is your path clearly marked by others who already know the way?

Once you start up that mountain, your heart must be steadfast, because there are no easy places to turn around and head back down to relative safety. But as those who have reached the summit and lived to tell about it, let us assure you it is worth the risk, worth the work, and worth the preparation.

The view from the top is breathtaking!

Tim and Heidi Guthrie

Part I:

Pathway
For
The Journey

Day 1
Choose Today

Joshua 24:15 "...choose for yourselves today whom you will serve: whether the gods which your fathers served which were beyond the River, or the gods of the Amorites in whose land you are living; but as for me and my house, we will serve the LORD."

Why is it that we so often think of God as merely a divine being and not a divine destination? In our culture of half-hearted, easily dropped commitments, we so often find those willing to claim God as their personal Savior while those same people take issue with God's ways of doing things – His Lordship in their lives. Our churches are filled with those who say they love God, but whose daily choices reflect that they would rather follow their own path.

At the beginning of this journey of personal revival, you must make a choice. Are you willing to follow God's directions to find your way to faithfulness? It is not enough to give lip-service to an idea or let the current of common thought pull you along. You must decide. You must choose. If you choose God, it can not be for the purpose of having a divine being to adore when it suits you, but God as your ultimate destination; your habitation.

Before you take a single step, you need to know where you are headed. And as Joshua knew, the time to decide is TODAY. Do not wait – choose your path while you are able.

Daily Journal – Day 1

How do you view God? Do you see Him as a 'backup plan' for the times when life deals harshly with you, or is God your Plan A, your goal, and the prize at the end of your journey? Look carefully at your life: how do you spend your time, money and energies? What do you choose, today, as your goal in life…and why?

_____

_____

_____

_____

_____

_____

_____

_____

_____

_____

_____

_____

_____

_____

_____

_____

_____

_____

_____

_____

_____

Day 2
Where Are You?

*Gen 12:1 Now the LORD had said to Abram:
"Get out of your country, from your family and from your
father's house, to a land that I will show you."*

It would be wonderful if we could open up our Bible, and inside the front cover was a map of our life with a little orange triangle stating "You Are Here." Life is a journey with an ultimate destination – Heaven – but there are many shorter milestones and mountains we reach for along the way. The first step in choosing the right pathway to where you need to go is in knowing where you are.

Abram's destination was uncertain, but he knew where he was. He was in a position of complete surrender and obedience to the will of God. When the LORD said "Go," Abram went. God's only direction was a rather vague, "I will show you." Was Abram uncertain of what he would find when he finally arrived? Of course. Did that keep him from stepping out in faith? Of course not.

You are on a personal journey of discovery and commitment. The vision has been cast, and preparation is being made to forge a way through the wilderness. But where are you? Are you in fellowship with God, so that you know you can confidently take your next step toward Him without going off course? Before you move a muscle, know that you can find your tiny triangle labeled: You Are Here.

Daily Journal – Day 2

Where are you in your spiritual journey? Are you surrendered to God's way, regardless of your own desires, or are you holding on to unconfessed sin, wanting to keep to your own path? Write your thoughts in the space below.

_____

_____

_____

_____

_____

_____

_____

_____

_____

_____

_____

_____

_____

_____

_____

_____

_____

_____

_____

_____

_____

_____

Day 3
On the Way

Matt 15:32 Now Jesus called His disciples ...and said, "I have compassion on the multitude, because they have now continued with Me three days...and I do not want to send them away hungry, lest they faint on the way."

Three days does not seem like much, in the great scheme of things, but when you are tired, hungry, thirsty, in pain, or stressed out, three days can seem like forever. Ask any CPA about the three days before Tax Day, or a retailer about the three days before Christmas, or a Choir Director about three days before Easter Cantata. Ask an overdue mother if three days matters or ask yourself how Mary Magdalene felt three days before Christ's resurrection. Talk about forever!

On this third day of your journal journey, do you already feel the bruises of spiritual warfare? Are you hungry for peace, for relief, or for a sign that everything is going to come out all right? Never fear, dear friend, because provisions are on the way. For those of you who are just plodding along trying to continue step by step with Jesus, rest assured He has compassion for you. He will not send you away hungry.

There will be times along this journey that you may feel a bit faint, but remember that Jesus is standing by with food enough for all. Just reach out to him, take what He offers, and you will be On Your Way in no time at all.

Daily Journal – Day 3

Are you on the way to your destination, but worrying a bit about provisions? Do you wonder if you will have the strength, the resources, or the spiritual understanding to go all the way? Take a few moments and write down your thoughts about Jesus' ability to provide what you need.

_____

_____

_____

_____

_____

_____

_____

_____

_____

_____

_____

_____

_____

_____

_____

_____

_____

_____

_____

_____

_____

Day 4
Take Heed

1 Corinthians 10:12 Therefore let him who thinks he stands take heed lest he fall.

Our teenaged son was acting out of character recently and praising himself for some (yes, we must admit) rather impressive basketball moves. We had a good laugh over his complete absence of modesty, but the laughter was followed with a loving reminder: take heed.

Do you ever find you have strained a muscle trying to pat yourself on the back after a spiritual victory? Perhaps you managed to get in a good habit of having daily 'quiet times' with God, or had perfect attendance in Bible Study, or gave more to the offering than usual. Did it make you feel as though you had 'arrived?' You are not alone in this. It is a common distraction. Read just one verse more, and you will see that our sins have lots of company.

The truth is: we must be on constant guard that we do not begin to think we have attained our spiritual summit. Every victory we achieve, no matter how small or great, belongs to the Lord and is reached through His patient grace.

Yesterday, you thought about where you are. Keep in mind that the path might be hard to follow if you are busy admiring yourself in the rearview mirror. Take Heed. The road may get bumpy.

Daily Journal – Day 4

Is it possible that there areas in your life in which you are 'spiritually haughty'? Do you ever find yourself being judgmental about how others behave, dress, or give? Be honest with yourself. God already knows the truth.

_____

_____

_____

_____

_____

_____

_____

_____

_____

_____

_____

_____

_____

_____

_____

_____

_____

_____

_____

_____

Day 5
Lost and Found

Luke 15:4-7 "What man of you, having a hundred sheep, if he loses one of them, does not leave the ninety-nine in the wilderness, and go after the one which is lost until he finds it? And when he has found it, he lays it on his shoulders, rejoicing."

Being lost is a scary experience. Most of us, at one time or another, became separated from our parents during childhood. Perhaps it was in a busy shopping mall or amusement park; maybe it was just for a few seconds of panic, or for a few terrifying hours of confusion and despair. At any rate, it is an experience we would not like to repeat. And yet…

On this journey of life, do you find yourself lost and bewildered? Are you uncertain you are on the right path or on any path at all? Do you find yourself running blindly through the forest trying to find some hint that you are going in the right direction, only to realize you are going in circles? If this is you, remember what you have been taught: Stay calm…stand still…and wait for help to arrive.

In His incredible plan, God never intended for us to find our own way to Him. He asks only that we stop running from Him in our desperation, and trust that He will come to us. He left His throne, His home, and His every comfort to follow you into the dark and search for you until you were found. Stop running. Take the hand He's reaching out to you, and let yourself be Found.

Daily Journal – Day 5

Are you Lost? Are you uncertain of your final destination? The Bible tells us that we can know for sure that we belong to Jesus for eternity. If you are tired of the constant stomach-churning uncertainty, go call your Pastor right now, and tell him you have decided to stop running. If this is not you, then you are an official member of the search party. What are your plans to help the Savior reach those who are lost?

_____

_____

_____

_____

_____

_____

_____

_____

_____

_____

_____

_____

_____

_____

_____

_____

_____

_____

_____

Day 6
Do you want to be well?

John 5:2-9 ...and a certain man was there, who had been thirty-eight years in his sickness. When Jesus saw him lying there, and knew that he had already been a long time in that condition, he said to him, "Do you wish to get well?"

When we first surrendered our lives to the ministry, God moved us to a far land. It was not quite Timbuktu, Africa, but to us, a Texas boy and an Oklahoma girl, Southern Louisiana felt like the foreign mission field. Mom and Dad and brothers and sisters were a long way away, and our first move as newlyweds felt like we were going halfway around the world. God said "go" so we went, and we do not regret it.

To the handicapped man by the pool, the water might as well have been halfway around the world. He had long ago accepted that the journey was an impossible one. He believed he would die in his current condition within sight of his destination. Then, Jesus came along and changed his life.

Do you want God's best for you, or have you grown so comfortable with your life as it is that when given the opportunity, you will fight any change, even for the better? Are you content with *status quo,* even if there is room for improvement? It is your choice, either way, but there is only one way to wholeness...keep your eyes on Jesus, and when he gives the signal, take up your bed and walk.

Daily Journal – Day 6

Are you willing to get up and walk – to put forth some effort – to reach your destination? What, if anything, is holding you back? If you are willing to be well, to be whole spiritually, and to obediently follow Jesus daily, commit that to Him on the space below.

_____
_____
_____
_____
_____
_____
_____
_____
_____
_____
_____
_____
_____
_____
_____
_____
_____
_____
_____
_____
_____

Day 7
Are You Narrow-Minded?

Matthew 7:13-14 "Enter by the narrow gate; for wide is the gate and broad is the way that leads to destruction, and there are many who go in by it. Because narrow is the gate and difficult is the way which leads to life, and there are few who find it."

We recently came across a church markee that read, "Don't be too open-minded, your brains may leak out." It gave us a good laugh at first, but later it got us thinking. In our culture, open-mindedness about 'religion' is a virtue. Popular thought is that God, by any other name, is still God, and that there are many ways to get to Heaven or 'Nirvana.'

Unfortunately, popular thought is often wrong. In this case, the majority is dead wrong. Their way, we are told in Matthew, leads to destruction, even though the way is broad and easy. If you are finding that your spiritual walk is easy, that Christianity is a breeze, and that you have all the answers, you may want to recheck what road you are on, because that is not the way Jesus describes the way we should be going.

The narrow path requires a daily fight against temptation, discouragement, hardship and disillusionment, but it is the right way to go. When it gets tough, do not lose heart! Jesus successfully walked the Way of Suffering, so He is the perfect guide for your Narrow-Minded journey.

Daily Journal – Day 7

    Although the Christian walk should be full of joy, it is rarely comfortable. Are you facing daily trials and struggles? What indications do you have in your life that you are on the right path? List them below, and then spend some time praying and asking Jesus to guide you through, over or around them.

_____

_____

_____

_____

_____

_____

_____

_____

_____

_____

_____

_____

_____

_____

_____

_____

_____

_____

_____

_____

Day 8
Folly or Favor?

Proverbs 14:8-9 The wisdom of the prudent is to understand his way: but the folly of fools is deceit.
Fools make a mock at sin: but among the righteous there is favour.

We would all like to think we are wise. Watch any day or night time talk show and you will find a multitude of self-proclaimed experts on any given subject debating others with completely differing views. Occasionally, we will watch someone floundering in their attempt to argue a ridiculous point and one of us will get caught muttering, "Denial ain't just a river in Egypt, buddy." It is true, though. The folly of fools is deceit…in a word: denial. Most of the world makes a mockery of sin these days, and they foolishly believe there will be no repercussions.

So, how do you understand God's way and avoid foolishness? The key to the map is in verse 9: righteousness. Simply doing what is right. Not in our own eyes, but in God's. The 'right' move for any given situation is clearly spelled out in Scripture. Just take Proverbs, for example; it covers everything from work ethic, to marital relationships, to child rearing and lending money. It is full of instruction on how to act righteously in hundreds of situations. The question is: do you want to know what is right, or do you want to live in denial. If it is denial, you may drown in it.

Daily Journal – Day 8

How do you look at sin? Do you find yourself laughing with it in on a daily basis? Do the things that you read, watch, and listen to make lighthearted fun of sin, or do they encourage you to do what is right before God? Honestly evaluate how much time you spend on folly vs. God's favor, and list those things that need to change in your daily habits:

_____
_____
_____
_____
_____
_____
_____
_____
_____
_____
_____
_____
_____
_____
_____
_____
_____
_____
_____
_____

Day 9
Trust Issues

Proverbs 3:5-6 Trust in the LORD with all your heart,
And lean not on your own understanding;
In all your ways acknowledge Him,
And He shall direct your paths.

If you have not noticed, trust is in short supply these days. Prime Time is full of so-called 'reality' shows in which the purpose of the hour's entertainment is 'win at all costs.' The cameramen always seem to be ready to catch the backstabbing, cheating, and double-dealing dished out to opponents and teammates alike, and the world revels in it.

Which of us has not been betrayed by someone we loved and trusted unwisely? Or which of us has not been guilty at one time or another of betraying someone's trust in us? We are, none of us, guiltless. None but One. None but Jesus.

We must be cautious, it is true, when choosing someone to confide in, but we must be equally cautious that we do not allow our past bad experiences to color our relationship with our Savior. When you begin to think you can rely only on yourself in this world, you have shut out the single source of true light, guidance, and security for your journey ahead. The One called 'Faithful and True' can be trusted with your heart, your secrets, your fears, and with every step you take in life. Trust Him today, and He will direct your path.

Daily Journal – Day 9

    Do you have trust issues? Have you been hurt in the past by someone you believed would never betray you? Most importantly, have these experiences caused you to be hesitant in trusting even the Lord with your most secret hopes and dreams, with your daily decisions and trials? Search your heart, and then list three things in your life that you are certain you need to trust the Lord with today:

_____

_____

_____

_____

_____

_____

_____

_____

_____

_____

_____

_____

_____

_____

_____

_____

_____

_____

Day 10
The Way

John 14:5-6 Thomas said to Him, "Lord, we do not know where You are going, and how can we know the way?" Jesus said to him, "I am the way, the truth, and the life. No one comes to the Father except through Me."

We have spent the past nine days discussing the pathway for our journey. We have learned that the road is narrow and difficult, fraught with trials and false, easy trails. You have been encouraged to choose your path, and to have the courage to search your heart and look honestly at where you are in your spiritual walk. You have been warned to 'take heed' not to trust too much in yourself, and encouraged to trust everything to Jesus to guide your way.

So, how can you be certain that Jesus can be trusted to guide you on your journey? How can you know that He knows the way? Because, dear friend, He *is* The Way.

The right path is not so difficult to find if one is sincerely open to finding it, because the pathway is not a treasure map with an X marking the spot. The pathway is a person. Your path is your relationship with Jesus Christ. If you are burdened by indecision or insecurity, today is the day for you to drop that burden, and to take Jesus by the hand in complete trust with every aspect of your life. The road ahead will not always be easy, but it will be worth it…all The Way there.

Daily Journal – Day 10

Are you convinced yet of your complete inability to guide your own path? If so, then you are right where you need to be in your journey. The little orange triangle marked You Are Here should be stamped firmly at the foot of the cross. If it is, then you are ready to take your next step. What have you learned in the past ten days that has given you the assurance that you are headed in the right direction? Write your thoughts below, and then get ready to strap on your pack! The journey is about to get interesting!

_____

_____

_____

_____

_____

_____

_____

_____

_____

_____

_____

_____

_____

_____

_____

_____

Part II:

Provisions
For
The Journey

Day 11
1st Provision: Your Cross

Luke 14:27 And whoever does not bear his cross and come after Me cannot be My disciple.

When preparing for a long, difficult journey, the first rule is usually 'pack light.' It is important for us to know, that the same principle is true with our Spiritual Luggage. Did you notice that Jesus did not tell us to bear *His* cross? He already took care of that one. It is a good thing, too, because the weight of it would crush us.

So, what is your cross, and how much does it weigh? It, quite simply, is the shape and weight of your sacrifice. In the previous verse, Jesus tells us that we must be willing to lay everything down for Him: every member of our family, and even our life. In Luke 14:33, He tells us we must be willing to forsake all we have in order to follow Him.

Does this cross seem a burden too heavy to bear? In Matthew 11:30, did Jesus not tell us His yoke is easy and His burden is light? He did not lie! Because, my fellow traveler, in order to pick up this cross of sacrifice, we must lay down every other burden in our lives that we are trying to carry on our own: our families, our friends, our personal possessions and cares, even our own hopes and dreams. So, your cross is as light as air. Lay it all down. There is freedom in casting the weight of responsibility onto the sturdy shoulders of your Guide, and taking up your very own cross.

Daily Journal – Day 11

Are you carrying more weight on your shoulders than Jesus expects you to carry? Are you taking on responsibilities that are the Lord's to bear? Are you trying to carry your family, your job, your church, or your reputation? Below, list those burdens that are weighing you down…and then lay them down where you stand. Jesus' pack can hold them.

_____

_____

_____

_____

_____

_____

_____

_____

_____

_____

_____

_____

_____

_____

_____

_____

_____

_____

Day 12
2nd Provision – Light

Ps 119:104-105 Through Your precepts I get understanding;
Therefore I hate every false way.
Your word is a lamp to my feet and a light to my path.

When you first became a Christian, did you feel that all of life had become illuminated, and you saw everything more clearly than you ever had? If you have been a Christian for a while, have you since walked through the valley of shadows a time or two? There are times in our Christian walk that we look up and realize that we have stepped off the path into darkness, or when we fall behind Jesus or even run on ahead of Him. When we do this, we lose our light, and our steps are sure to falter.

A few years ago as our family struggled through a succession of trials in our ministry and family, we began joking that every time we saw a light at the end of the tunnel, it turned out to be a locomotive bearing down on us. The truth we soon realized was that we had gotten caught up in doing the work of the ministry, but without the illumination we needed to be truly effective. We were trying to run on ahead on our own, and were not walking in the daily light of our relationship with Christ.

He is the Way, but He is also the lamp for our feet. To spot pitfalls, false trails, or stumbling blocks, we must stay within touching distance of our Guide. Keep His Word open and near, and let it Light your journey.

Daily Journal – Day 12

Has keeping up with these daily devotions been a struggle to you? Do you find yourself sometimes in a dark tunnel, not sure if the light up ahead is going to guide you or run you over? If so, just keep pressing on and reading God's Word. Make time for it daily, no matter what else you have going on in your busy life. Take a moment to skim over Psalm 119 right now, and write down three promises given to you when you spend time reading your Bible. How do these promises motivate you?

_____

_____

_____

_____

_____

_____

_____

_____

_____

_____

_____

_____

_____

_____

_____

_____

_____

_____

Day 13
3rd Provision – Food and Water

John 4:34 Jesus said to them, "My food is to do the will of Him who sent Me, and to finish His work."

Food plays an important part in our lives. Between church fellowships, dinners with friends, and the daily challenge of keeping two teenaged boys and their buddies filled up, we keep our active grocery list in a prominent place. We are also traveling a lot these days, and we have learned that when traveling, it becomes a bit more difficult to find good meals along the way; to look ahead and know where sustenance will come from. Our only guarantee is to pack a lunch and go prepared.

It is just as important to be fed on our spiritual journey. Have you noticed how often Jesus spoke of food and water? He realized it was a daily need that people could easily relate to, so He translated the filling of our spiritual life with the filling of our stomachs. Jesus stayed filled up on His journey by doing the will of God, and finishing His work. It is no different for us. If you are going to be sustained and replenished along your journey, you will need to be actively doing the Lord's will. His work is what it has always been: find the lost, reach out to those on the wrong path, and offer them the living water and the bread of life. The fountain is everlasting and the picnic basket is always full, so share it freely along the way. There is more than enough to go around.

Daily Journal – Day 13

Do you hunger along your journey? Just do God's will and you will be fed – it is a renewable resource, an over-flowing basket of sustaining strength. Do you see the lost around you who are dehydrated by the heat of their hopeless eternity? Are you going to determine to reach those on the journey to nowhere with the hope of living water? If so, what is your plan to reach out to them?

_____

_____

_____

_____

_____

_____

_____

_____

_____

_____

_____

_____

_____

_____

_____

_____

_____

_____

Day 14
4th Provision – Salt

Colossians 4:5-6 Walk in wisdom toward those who are outside, redeeming the time. Let your speech always be with grace, seasoned with salt, that you may know how you ought to answer each one.

Of course we need food and water for a journey, but is salt truly a necessity? Yes! It is not a luxury item, but a needed provision. Salt helps our bodies hold more water to prevent dehydration. It also acts as a preservative to keep food from spoiling. Lastly, it can be a delightful seasoning and make our food more enjoyable.

As you already know, the journey is a long one. You do not want to become faint from heat along the journey, nor do you want to eat food that has become rotten. But one of the most difficult attacks on our spiritual walk, because it is so easily disguised, is – let us be honest - boredom. All too soon, if we forget to be delighted daily in God's goodness and revel in the excitement of His revelations to us, our walk can become stale, stagnant and unpalatable. During those times, we find ourselves searching the roadsides for a little 'spice', and invariably become poisoned. Even worse, we make becoming 'saved' sound uninteresting to those we meet along our way.

We allow this to happen when we forget to meditate on and tell others about the exciting and wonderful goodness of God! Pour on the Salt!

Daily Journal – Day 14

Has the Christian walk become a bit boring or routine to you? Have you forgotten the excitement of your first discovery of Christ, or the thrill of His working in your life? Psalm 34:8 tells us to "taste and see that the Lord is good!" Below, make a list of the miraculous things God has done in your life since you first came to know Him. Then, tell someone today about at least one of those things.

_____

_____

_____

_____

_____

_____

_____

_____

_____

_____

_____

_____

_____

_____

_____

_____

_____

_____

Day 15
5th Provision - Utility Belt

Ephesians 6:14 Stand therefore, having girded your waist with truth…

The study of a Christian's armor cannot be truly understood without being familiar with the purposes of specific pieces of armor. Paul used the Roman soldiers' armor for his model.

The soldier's belt was made of thick leather wide enough to cover a large portion of his waist, and it served several purposes. First and foremost, it gave back support. Each soldier wielded a heavy sword and shield. This sturdy strip of leather would lend strength to his lower back. Secondly, it served as a utility belt, in which he could carry both weapons and tools. It would not only carry a sword and daggers, but the stone with which to sharpen them, and other necessary items. The third purpose is not as obvious until we recall that the soldier would wear a long robe that served as protection against the elements, and was his blanket at night. This robe, necessary as it was, could be a problem in battle, so the soldier would grab the hem of his robe and tuck it up inside his belt to get it out of his way.

What is truth? Simply, it is knowledge of God's Word. Knowing His Word gives you daily protection. Only the Truth will give you strength for your battles, access to your tools, and will also keep you from being tripped up in battle. So, strap on your belt!

Daily Journal – Day 15

Is your belt on? Do you keep it on, day and night, as the Roman soldiers did, or do you just rush to find it on that dusty shelf when you come under sudden attack? To know truth, you must study ahead, or when the battle comes to you, it will be too late to prepare. Do you have daily Bible study goals? If so, take them to the next level. If not, set a daily goal for yourself. It can be an amount of time, or certain number of verses. In the space below, commit these goals to God. Be specific. Finish this sentence: "Every day, I will study…"

_____

_____

_____

_____

_____

_____

_____

_____

_____

_____

_____

_____

_____

_____

_____

_____

_____

Day 16
6th Provision – Body Armor

Ephesians 6:14 ...having put on the breastplate of righteousness...

Every piece of armor is essential, but this one in particular can protect you from a killing blow. As every soldier knows, the loss of a limb can disqualify him from service, but he can most often continue to live without it. The breastplate, though, was for the sole purpose of protecting the vital organs in the chest and stomach area from fatal attacks. One piercing blow to the heart, and he was 'done for.'

Notice, if you will, that the verse does not tell us to put on the breastplate of *our* righteousness. Trust me, friend, you do not want that. Ours is full of holes! The righteousness of Christ has no tears, holes, or places worn thin from sin. It is one hundred percent completely impenetrable!

At the moment of salvation, God saw His Son's holiness on you, and He still does. Your adversary will try to convince you that you are weak and unholy, but it is just not true. Christ's blood covers ALL your sin. Satan's strongest, and most often used weapons against you are guilt and shame. He will remind you of past sins, try to tempt you into present sins, and convince you that you have no hope against future sins. These lies strike at your very heart and steal your breath. Put on Christ's Righteousness and stand strong against him!

Daily Journal – Day 16

Do you ever feel weakened by guilt and shame? When you lose a skirmish with sin, do you lose heart and walk away from the battlefield feeling unworthy and defeated? This is a battle tactic of our enemy, and you must determine not to let it work! Have you been putting on your own righteousness, and getting stabbed as a result? Take a few moments to look up the following verses, and write down some thoughts on how you can use these verses to help put on Christ's righteousness:

I John 4:4

_____
_____
_____
_____
_____
_____
_____
_____

Romans 1:17

_____
_____
_____
_____
_____
_____
_____
_____

Day 17
7th Provision – Adequate Footwear

*Ephesians 6:15 …and having shod your feet with the
preparation of the gospel of peace…*

Have you ever tried to walk a long distance in a
pair of uncomfortable shoes? In our family, fashion
often takes second place to comfort when it comes
to footwear. We have discovered that a pair of bad
shoes can make the entire body hurt. They can tire
us out, distract us from our work, and generally ruin
a good time. Taking a long journey or going into
battle with ill-fitting shoes does not work.

Paul knew that the Roman soldiers' footwear
was specially designed for long war campaigns and
fierce battles. They consisted of several layers of
padded leather with metal cleats or spikes attached
to the sole for traction. The shoes were attached
with long leather strips which wound around the
foot, ankle and calf. They were strong enough to
hold tight, but flexible enough for ease of
movement during fighting. Without proper
footwear, the soldier was of no use.

What do your feet have to do with the gospel?
Evangelism, my friend. We must prepare our feet
to 'Go and tell.' Did you know that sharing the
gospel is actually a defense against Satan? When
you are prepared to share the good news, you will
be nimble, quick, and surefooted against Satan's
attacks! Put on your walking shoes, and be
prepared to go!

Daily Journal – Day 17

How much time have you spent lately in preparing yourself to share the gospel? It really is not as difficult as you might think. Have you been saved? If so, you can share! You can prepare by studying, or even memorizing key scriptures about salvation (i.e. Romans 3:23; 5:8; 6:23; 8:38-39; 10:9-10, 13). Another important way to prepare to share is to write out your personal 'testimony' – the details about how and when you first came to know Jesus. Write out your testimony below:

_____

_____

_____

_____

_____

_____

_____

_____

_____

_____

_____

_____

_____

_____

_____

Now that you have your shoes on, walk with confidence, and share the Good News as you go!!

Day 18
8th Provision – Shield

Ephesians 6:16 ...above all, taking the shield of faith with which you will be able to quench all the fiery darts of the wicked one.

The Roman soldier's shield was made of tough leather over metal. It was usually about 4½ feet tall by 2½ feet in width. One of the major war tactics of the time was to shoot arrows tipped with flaming tar, so you can see why it would be so important for a soldier to be able to crouch down behind his shield to keep this fiery pitch from splattering on him. The arrow would either bounce off his shield, or get stuck in it and eventually burn itself out.

We know that our enemy, the wicked one, loves throwing fiery arrows. He is vicious and brutal, and likes nothing more than to inflict as much pain and agony against us as possible. He uses lies to discourage us, he tempts us in our personal areas of weakness, and he tries to make us afraid so we will be ineffective against him. You have likely felt the sting of his fiery darts when your shield was down. We have been there. It hurts.

So often when we come under attack, we turn and run. When that happens, we only get shot in the back. Satan has no honor in battle. Our Shield of Faith is the awesome reminder that God IS our shield against our enemy. His protection is total! Nothing gets by Him! When the arrows fly, have Faith and get behind God!

Daily Journal – Day 18

As God taught the Israelites to do, one of the best ways to build our faith is to set up visible reminders in our lives of what He has done for us in the past. It could be a timeline dating moments that you came through accidents or illnesses, a journal detailing God's hand in your spiritual walk, a plaque with your salvation birthday on it, or maybe a picture of a miracle child. Below, list times in your life when you knew God's hand was working in your life, and then determine a way to make some of those memories visible to you daily:

_____

_____

_____

_____

_____

_____

_____

_____

_____

_____

_____

_____

_____

_____

_____

_____

Day 19
9th Provision – Headgear

Ephesians 6:17 And take the helmet of salvation…

Soldiers know that to go into battle without a helmet is suicide. The slightest blow to your head can disorient. The smallest pieces of shrapnel can kill. As you have heard it said: "A mind is a terrible thing to waste." Our mind is the control center for our entire body. It controls our reflexes, our vital organs, and our thoughts. We cannot function on even the most basic level without our brain in tact.

Our mind is also the control center for our spiritual walk. This is why Satan so brutally and relentlessly attacks our minds! He knows that if he can get a blow in, he can completely disorient us and put us out of commission.

What is the helmet of salvation? As Paul is speaking specifically to those he knows are Christians, we must understand that it is not merely referring to the act of being saved. It is, rather, referring to the way we can use the fact of our salvation to protect our thoughts. One of Satan's greatest weapons against us is doubt. If he can convince us that Christ's work was not enough or confuse us about whether we are truly saved, he can disorient us and make us ineffective. When you remind Satan of the completeness of Christ's work of salvation in your life, his blows will become ineffective. So, put on your Helmet! Your mind is a battlefield!

Daily Journal – Day 19

Are you confused and uncertain about your salvation? When an invitation is given, do you worry whether you somehow got 'it' wrong the first time? You can and you must be certain, or you will never be able to function to your potential as a Christian! When the Bible tells us in Philippians 2:12 to 'work out our salvation' with fear and trembling, it is not telling us to work for it, but rather to do whatever it takes to get it nailed down once and for all. What does John 5:13 tell us about our salvation? Rewrite the verse in your own words below, and show how you will apply it:

_____

_____

_____

_____

_____

_____

_____

_____

_____

_____

_____

_____

_____

_____

_____

_____

_____

Day 20
10th Provision – Sword

Ephesians 6:17 ...and the sword of the Spirit, which is the word of God.

Keep in mind that Paul stresses the importance of putting *all* our armor on. Leaving even one piece off will leave you vulnerable to an expert sniper or bowman who has studied your weaknesses! If you leave off *any* of the previous provisions, you will be setting yourself up for defeat.

Now, as for your sword...this one is spelled out for us: the Word of God. We have seen already that the Word can give light and can serve as protection, but Christians are missing the primary use for the Word in our lives! It is an *offensive* weapon! Sadly, we have become a culture of defensive, fraidy-cat Christians who are not quite certain what we believe, or are too insecure to try to convince others we are right. We spend our time trying to hide from the attacks of the enemy rather than go after him with our sword raised in battle cry. Do you know why this is so tragic?

Well, why not take a few hours to study up in the Bible about the defensive armor of Satan? Do not bother - it is a waste of time. Why? BECAUSE HE DOES NOT HAVE ANY! Most Christians have never learned this truth! We hide or run away from an enemy that has a multitude of weapons but not one single defense against the two-edged Sword! Attack!!

Daily Journal – Day 20

Is Satan's lack of defense a new concept for you? When we learned it, it revolutionized how we looked at his attacks against us. So often now when we face the enemy, we are able to chase him away! James 4:7 tells us "resist the devil, and he will flee from you." There is no verse that more clearly shows us who should be afraid of the battles we encounter! Not us, but our enemy! Below, write a prayer to God asking for a greater understanding of how you can use the Word as an offensive weapon, and ask for the boldness to wield it in battle:

_____
_____
_____
_____
_____
_____
_____
_____
_____
_____
_____
_____
_____
_____
_____
_____
_____

Part III:

Power
For
The Journey

Day 21
Traveling Companions

Hebrews 10:24-25 And let us consider one another in order to stir up love and good works, not forsaking the assembling of ourselves together...but exhorting one another.

There is strength in numbers. First, God made Eve for Adam, to help and support him on his life journey. Then, as their family grew, God ordained the church as an even larger support group. The church, as full of idiosyncrasies as it is, is given to us as a source of strength. The very purpose of the church is to empower us on our journey. We all need someone watching our back and helping when we stumble.

This thing called The Church is often a mystery. Only God could put together so many fallible, sinful humans with only one thing in common, and make their 'assembly' a living testament to His goodness. Fortunately, we do not have to explain it. We only have to trust God and be obedient. As frustrated as we have become at times in the past with certain people or situations at church, we know that our church family has often been the only thing keeping us from complete collapse. We have often heard Christians – suffering grief, illness, or other serious trials – say, "I don't know how people make it without their church." The truth? Many do not.

You can trust God's Word about His church. Do not try to walk the journey alone. Let your traveling companions lend you strength on the way.

Daily Journal – Day 21

How do you view your involvement in church? Is it optional and just based on whether you are in the mood to attend, or do you faithfully attend every chance you get? Do you think only about what you can get from church, or do you also think about what you can contribute? This is your opportunity to spend some time meditating on your personal involvement and attitude in your church. After thinking about it, list three areas below in which you can improve your faithfulness and participation:

_____

_____

_____

_____

_____

_____

_____

_____

_____

_____

_____

_____

_____

_____

_____

_____

Day 22
The Joy of the Lord

Nehemiah 8:10 Go your way...for this day is holy to our Lord. Do not sorrow, for the joy of the LORD is your strength.

You may have already noticed, but we often tend to use lightheartedness when we deal with serious issues. We pray that we never come across as irreverent or uncaring. It is just the opposite, in fact. We have become so certain of the Lord's unconditional love for us and His ability to control any situation that we are able to relax in His goodness and find moments of laughter while we live in a spirit of joy.

Keep in mind that we are not talking about happiness. The root word of happiness, after all, is 'happen' - it is based on circumstance. If we allow our emotions to flow based on what 'happens' in life, we will be doomed to constant depression. Life is a perilous journey, with trials around every corner. Joy, however, is constant. Joy is an attitude of confidence in the Lord's ultimate victory and abiding care for us. Joy is, quite truthfully, a command. Paul tells us *twice* in Philippians 4:4 to rejoice and it is not qualified by the words "if you feel like it."

Do you feel weak? Discouraged? Defeated? Do you want power in your Christian walk? Just rejoice! Get your focus on God and off your circumstances, and you will find strength for your journey that you never knew you had!

Daily Journal – Day 22

On a scale from one to ten, how would you rate your daily joy? Is it a struggle? Do you find yourself slipping into a habit of pessimism or become easily discouraged? Life can be a joy-ride! Just make up your mind that you are going to be strong in the Lord through a conscious attitude of joy, and ask for His daily strength. For starters, take some time and list your blessings – as many as you can fit on the page:

_____

_____

_____

_____

_____

_____

_____

_____

_____

_____

_____

_____

_____

_____

_____

_____

_____

_____

Day 23
He is with you!

Psalm 23:4 Yea, though I walk through the valley of the shadow of death, I will fear no evil; For You are with me; Your rod and Your staff, they comfort me.

There is little doubt that along your journey, you are going to encounter a valley or two. Sometimes making our way up the mountain requires a few unexpected drops in elevation that can be dark and scary. You may even find grief or despair there, and wonder how you will ever resume your climb. Do not fear. God is with you. He is able.

Earlier, we put great emphasis on keeping your focus on the light of Jesus and staying near Him, but we also must point out that even in the darkness, God knows where you are. He can find you in the deepest shadows, and His rod can prod you back in the right direction while His staff wraps around you and lifts you up. You are not alone. Satan will whisper to you that you are alone, that God has left you, and that there is no hope. He is lying.

There is no greater power and confidence than knowing your Heavenly Father is with you. He is acting not only as your guide, but as your security detail. When you can not see to find your way, just trust that He can see the path back up the mountain. He is not afraid. He can not be shaken by doubt or discouragement. Take comfort in knowing that He will never, ever leave you or forsake you, and let that solid truth give you power beyond imagination!

Daily Journal – Day 23

There may be times that you do not feel God is near. Perhaps you have had a major disappointment or grief in your life that does not seem fair. Or maybe you have allowed unconfessed sin to interfere with your daily fellowship with God. How do you respond during these moments? How should the understanding that God is always with you alter how you respond?

_____

_____

_____

_____

_____

_____

_____

_____

_____

_____

_____

_____

_____

_____

_____

_____

_____

_____

Day 24
Amazing Gracefulness

2 Samuel 22:33-34 God is my strength and power, and He makes my way perfect. He makes my feet like the feet of deer, and sets me on my high places.

Our family has a few claims to fame, but gracefulness is not one of them. Heidi has a way of tripping over invisible obstacles, Tim runs on the softball field as though he is in three feet of water, and our oldest, Timothy, has not met a staircase he has not managed to fall up or down. Nathan's lack of gracefulness is more in his ability to say the wrong thing in one of those moments when an entire room has suddenly become quiet. We have learned to laugh at our fallibility in a multitude of areas, and we are in a daily process of learning how amazing it is that God still manages to use us.

When God tells us that He will make our way perfect, we must know this is not a promise to make *us* perfect. We will not be perfect this side of Heaven. What it does mean is that He will use us in the perfect way, even with all our imperfections, and that His power will overcome our limitations.

If you are trying to scramble up that precarious perch of perfection on your own, or if someone else has placed you up on a pedestal, you are very likely to trip and fall and get hurt. Only when God picks you up and puts your feet on those high places can you truly feel His grace and gracefulness. Walking in His perfection is the only true position of power.

Daily Journal – Day 24

Do you find yourself trying to be perfect in front of others? Because of your imperfections or personal struggles, do you lack of confidence in your ability to be an effective minister for God? Look up the following verses and answer the questions given:

Genesis 12:12-13. What did Abram do wrong here?

_____

_____

Exodus 4:10. What was Moses self-conscious about?

_____

_____

II Samuel 11:3-4. What was David's sin?

_____

_____

Luke 22:54-62. What do you think was the reason for Peter's denial of Jesus?

_____

_____

Hebrews 11:31. What was Rahab's profession before she allowed God to use her?

_____

If God used them, He can use you! Pray and ask God for the confidence to make yourself available.

Day 25
Power That Works

Ephesians 3:17-21 That you…may be able to comprehend…what is the width and length and depth and height — to know the love of Christ which passes knowledge; that you may be filled with all the fullness of God. Now to Him who is able to do exceedingly abundantly above all that we ask or think, according to the power that works in us…

What exactly is the power that works in us? In order to know, we must first attempt to comprehend the incomprehensible love of Christ. The clues Paul gives us here are just a jumping off point in our feeble understanding of how much God loves us.

Think of the *depths* Christ sunk in order to redeem us. No one could have gone lower than to have taken on the sins of mankind to such a total degree that God has to turn His face away in disgust (Eph.4:8-9). The *length* and *width* encompass Jesus' outstretched arms to remove our sins as far as the East is from the West (Psalm 103:12). The *height* is both our future gift of Heaven and also God's work in us right now. Can anyone truly grasp those dimensions? Just think: if Christ is in us, we are filled with *all* the fullness of God. The very Spirit that has gone to such great lengths to show us love is now inside our hearts!

If then, the power working and living within us is the very same power that conquered death and the grave, is it any wonder that God can do exceedingly abundantly above all that we ask or think? This is power for our journey, and it is without limits!

Daily Journal – Day 25

How often do you spend time considering the depth and length and width and height of God's love for you? Satan's greatest weapon is in using our mind to weaken us, but that same mind can lend us strength by reminding us who we are in Christ! Below, list a few specific things that you need power for in your daily life, and then write out your belief that God is able to do powerful things through His Spirit working in you:

_____

_____

_____

_____

_____

_____

_____

_____

_____

_____

_____

_____

_____

_____

_____

_____

_____

_____

Day 26
Look Out Stomach, Here It Comes!

Proverbs 18:20-21 A man's stomach shall be satisfied from the fruit of his mouth; from the produce of his lips he shall be filled. Death and life are in the power of the tongue, And those who love it will eat its fruit.

We have all heard the saying, "You will eat your words." Now we know where it came from. There are some so-called theologians in popular circles these days who teach that you can literally cause life or death with your words: that if you pray to not get sick, the devil will hear you and bring sickness based on your lack of faith. This is taking scripture out of context. How could any prayer of ours to God – who tells us to pray specifically and place all our needs and concerns before him – be corrupted or used against us? It can not. It is totally out of character for God to allow us to be harmed through our prayer life, and therefore it must be a false teaching. Besides that, we know that death and life are in His hands and under His control.

So, what does Proverbs 18 tell us about our words? That they are powerful, and that they can be either uplifting or damaging. Along our journey, we can choose to speak words that edify ourselves and turn others away from Jesus (spiritual death), or we can choose to speak the gospel of Christ to the lost and lead them to salvation (spiritual life). The scripture tells us that we will be filled with whatever we speak, but whether our words bring satisfaction or cause food poisoning is up to us.

Daily Journal – Day 26

What do you talk about? How do you speak to others? Does a majority of what you say edify and uplift and point others to Christ, or is there an absence of truly spiritual and life-giving conversation? Think about any conversations you had this past week in which you responded hurtfully with your words, or remained silent when you should have spoken. Below, write some ideas for how could you have responded differently:

_____

_____

_____

_____

_____

_____

_____

_____

_____

_____

_____

_____

_____

_____

_____

_____

_____

_____

_____

_____

Day 27
Treasure Chests

2 Corinthians 4:7-9 We have this treasure in earthen vessels that the excellence of the power may be of God and not of us. We are hard-pressed on every side, yet not crushed; we are perplexed, but not in despair; persecuted, but not forsaken; struck down, but not destroyed.

Our culture's renewed fascination with pirates has also sparked a new interest in treasure chests. Everyone knows that a treasure chest must be sturdy, airtight, and impenetrable. It must have a strong lock and be hidden away with only a single map marking the spot, right? If you are talking about earthly treasure, that is all certainly true. But as is the case in most everything, God's process is completely different. His ways are not ours.

God's treasure is in soft, penetrable vessels made of dirt and filled with holes and weak spots and rottenness. These vessels are not locked and hidden away with only a single, moth-eaten map to find the way. Rather, they are set out in the open on a hill and a multitude of maps are passed around the whole world to mark the spot. *We* are these vessels, and we contain the most priceless treasure of God.

To the world, this does not make a bit of sense at first. Why would a King entrust such a valuable treasure to such an inferior container? But the remarkable truth is that the treasure inside is the very power that holds it together! Our world needs to see that no feat of man, no pirate, and no power can break us apart…and that a cross marks the spot!

Daily Journal – Day 27

On this journey to faithfulness, it is a certainty that you will be hard-pressed, perplexed, persecuted and struck down. Sounds rough, huh? But God is able to protect the treasure He has entrusted to you, and people will see His glory through the very fact that you, in your weakness, are not crushed, in despair, forsaken or destroyed! Below, list some of your weak areas, and then list ways that God can be strong through them:

_____

_____

_____

_____

_____

_____

_____

_____

_____

_____

_____

_____

_____

_____

_____

_____

_____

Day 28
A Mighty Fortress

Psalm 18:2 The LORD is my rock and my fortress and my deliverer; My God, my strength , in whom I will trust; My shield and the horn of my salvation, my stronghold.

Years ago, we traveled to the wedding of some friends of ours. We arrived to enjoy the ceremony, but as we headed to our hotel afterward, we became disoriented in the dark and took a wrong turn. One of us (who will remain unnamed, although you can probably guess) saw no need to stop for directions until we were in an area in which it would have been foolhardy to have stopped for any reason. We were lost and running low on fuel in a city with a reputation for eating tourists alive. All we knew to do was pray as we drove down littered side-streets and shadowy back alleys. Within moments of crying out to God, we came upon a sign pointing us in the right direction, and found our hotel a short while later. Never had we been so glad to see a building! It was a bright and strong refuge for us!

This journey you have undertaken – this walk toward faithfulness – will be fraught with battles and obstacles, but you have the assurance of protection and rest along the way. Shelter is just around the corner. If you just ask for direction and watch for God's signs, His stronghold will be there for you to run to, and His protection will shield you in the midst of whatever you are dealing with in life. Our God is a mighty fortress. Run to Him and be safe!

Daily Journal – Day 28

Are you a worrier? Do you find yourself becoming nervous about your health, your family situation or your financial future? Does the prospect of terrorism or the deterioration of the moral values of our country make you fearful? If so, then just run into your stronghold and trust that you are safe within the fortress of God. List your fears below, and then write a prayer of commitment to remain in the safety of God's presence:

_____

_____

_____

_____

_____

_____

_____

_____

_____

_____

_____

_____

_____

_____

_____

_____

_____

_____

_____

Day 29
Powerless

Hosea 13:14 I will ransom them from the power of the grave;
I will redeem them from death.

Our 'demotion' to full-time pastoring following five years of youth ministry was a shock to our systems. In addition to the added responsibilities, we had an unexpected ministry opportunity presented to us: a multitude of funerals. It seemed the moment the job changed, everyone in our church (or in our pastorless sister-churches) who had suffered from a long-term illness decided to depart the earth within a matter of months. Many times, we were asked to perform and attend (Tim performed, Heidi attended) four or more funerals in one week. One Saturday, we had three funerals in succession in that single day. This pattern lasted for nearly six months. Do the math. It is shocking!

When we tell this story, we usually get the same reaction, with people saying, "How depressing!" Believe it or not, that was not the case. Rather, it was enlightening and freeing. We were fortunate to understand early in our ministry the immortal words of Jake Hess: Death Ain't No Big Deal. Although we had a few sad experiences with those whose final destination was uncertain, the majority of funerals were for Christians who had been ransomed from the power of the grave. When we truly understand that Jesus has redeemed us from death, a funeral is just a 'going away' party for a stage of our journey, and death becomes powerless!

Daily Journal – Day 29

What are your thoughts about death? Do you fear it? Do you try not to think about it at all? Most of the world is in denial about the subject. They would rather not have to think about eternity, so they fill their lives with distractions. As Christians, we have an important ministry to those who fear the grave. They are looking for hope, and assurance, and it is up to us to point the way! Take a few moments to write down your feelings about your own death. Are you afraid? Are you anxious? Are you ready?

_____

_____

_____

_____

_____

_____

_____

_____

_____

_____

_____

_____

_____

_____

_____

_____

Day 30
Limitless

Psalms 78:41-42 Yes, again and again they…limited the Holy One of Israel. They did not remember His power.

This verse really hits home for us, does it not? As we travel along on this journey to faithfulness, we put limitations on God, again and again. So often, we put God in a box and we customize our prayers based on what we think He will do, rather than on what we know He *can* do. Sometimes we are limited by our personal experience. We have all heard or said, "We've never done it that way before" or "I've never seen God do something like that", and we miss out on the new and surprising blessings He wants to bring into our lives.

The key here is not in looking back and remembering our personal experiences and limitations – the key is in looking at God's personal experiences and limitless power. As we mentioned before, God told the Israelites to set up monuments along their journey to remember what He had done for them. Think of just a few: He created the universe, He fashioned man out of dust, He saved mankind from the flood, He made a path through the Red Sea, He made the walls of Jericho tumble, He sent manna from Heaven to feed His people, and He sent His Son to save all people, just to name a few. We make God too small in our minds because we do not think enough about His power! Again and again, we must remember who He is, because the only limit to God's power is our memory!

Daily Journal – Day 30

How do you limit God in your life? Do you lack faith in a certain area? Perhaps you already think you know what God's answer will be to a certain prayer, so you do not give Him a chance to work. Or maybe you focus more on the disappointments in your life than the way God has come through for you in miraculous and powerful ways. Take a few moments to list things in your life and the life of your church that you want God to do…things that ONLY God can do, and then pray in faith, believing His power is limitless:

_____

_____

_____

_____

_____

_____

_____

_____

_____

_____

_____

_____

_____

_____

_____

_____

Part IV:

Purpose
For
The Journey

Day 31
Purpose Driven God

Proverbs 19:21 There are many plans in a man's heart,
Nevertheless the LORD's counsel — that will stand.

Everywhere we go today, we hear about how important it is to find our purpose. There are a multitude of career guides, personality profiles, and self-help books designed to guide us toward finding purpose in life and reaching our personal goals. This is all fine and good, as long as our personal goals are in line with God's goals; as long as our purpose is His purpose.

In making plans to our heart's content, we forget that Jeremiah 17:9 tells us the heart is deceitful above all things and desperately wicked. If we 'listen to' our heart the way so many feel-good movies and television shows counsel us to do these days, we are sure to end up in a mess. When our heart leads us away from God's counsel, we can know we are headed in the wrong direction. Sometimes even in doing 'ministry-minded' things, we can become self-driven and forget the true reason behind what we are doing.

God never does anything willy-nilly or based on whim or emotion. He has a plan, and it will stand the test of eternity. Rather than make plans in your heart, you must seek out the plans in God's heart. Then, when you are in fellowship with God and daily seeking His counsel will you truly have a driving purpose that will stand.

Daily Journal – Day 31

Do you seek to know God's purpose and plans on a daily basis? Are your current life and ministry goals in line with what is in God's heart? Take a few moments and write out what you believe God's short and long-term purposes are for you, and truly seek His counsel about any adjustments you need to make in your life or attitudes:

_____

_____

_____

_____

_____

_____

_____

_____

_____

_____

_____

_____

_____

_____

_____

_____

_____

_____

_____

_____

_____

Day 32
Intents and Purposes

Genesis 50:20 But as for you, you meant evil against me; but God meant it for good.

There is nothing we love more than to see Satan's schemes backfire on him. Take the cross, for example. The devil thought killing Jesus was the way to stop God's plan to save mankind, and yet that death was the very thing that set us free and gave us victory over the grave. Ironic, is it not?

In Genesis 37, we see Joseph sold into slavery by his jealous brothers. Later, he was imprisoned and then eventually put into a position to interpret Pharoah's dreams. Satan must have seen young Joseph's promise and dedication to God, but instead of hindering God's purpose, his evil plans allowed Joseph to become second in command of all Egypt and save millions of people. Joe's trials would have been enough to make any reasonable person bitter, but he had wisdom beyond his years. He knew that God had an ultimate purpose for his life, and the pain was just a part of the journey in getting there.

Pain and betrayal are a part of your journey and ours. All of us have experienced this in some way. You may even be in the middle of it right now. When the attacks come, insidious voices whisper lies that tell you God has forgotten or abandoned you. Do not believe it. God is just allowing you to be placed in the position of greatest effectiveness. God's purposes are always for our good!

Daily Journal – Day 32

When attacks or trials come, what are your first thoughts? Do you become bitter and discouraged immediately, or do you ask God to open your eyes to what He is doing? Below, list two trials in your life that God has used to allow you to minister to others. If you are in the middle of one, write down two ways God may use this now or in the future to help someone else. Then, thank God for turning Satan's tables against Him and ask for wisdom to trust Him the way Joseph did!

_____

_____

_____

_____

_____

_____

_____

_____

_____

_____

_____

_____

_____

_____

_____

_____

_____

Day 33
Darkness to Light

Acts 26:16-18 But rise and stand on your feet; for I have appeared to you for this purpose, to make you a minister and a witness… to open their eyes, in order to turn them from darkness to light.

There is no question that we are living in a harsh world. To climb the ladder of success, the theme is 'everyone for his self.' Fortunately, we can live in this world and not be of it. We can rise and stand in the middle of it and still fulfill our purpose.

We talked about darkness and light a few weeks ago and discussed how easy it is to stray off the path and get lost in the shadows when we get our eyes off Christ. Not wandering off into danger is important for our personal journey, but what if staying right in the middle of the road is all you ever accomplish? What if you never reach out a hand or shine a light on those who are mired in the mud and darkness along the wrong paths?

Just as we read in Ephesians 6 regarding the armor, we again see reference to 'standing.' Keep in mind this does not suggest standing around doing nothing, but rather standing firm; much in the way you might stand in a tug of war competition, digging in your feet and bracing yourself. When our feet are planted and we have God as our anchor, we can reach out to those who are lost and blind, and gently pull them onto the right path to join us both in our journey and in fulfilling our purpose!

Daily Journal – Day 33

We hope you feel stronger and better equipped for your journey than you did 33 days ago. Our prayer is that your feet would be firmly planted with God as your anchor, and that you would have the strength to stand firm as you achieve your purpose. Below, list five people (no one in your household who may read this and be offended) who could use a helping hand to safety. They could be family members, acquaintances, friends or co-workers God has placed in your life for you to minister to or share the gospel with. Then, write a prayer committing to God that you will stand for them:

_____

_____

_____

_____

_____

_____

_____

_____

_____

_____

_____

_____

_____

_____

_____

_____

Day 34
Eternal Purpose

Ephesians 3:10-11... that now the manifold wisdom of God might be made known by the church to the principalities and powers in the heavenly places, according to the eternal purpose which He accomplished in Christ Jesus our Lord...

You have probably heard the old joke that a camel is a 'horse designed by a church committee.' It is okay to laugh at ourselves sometimes – to smile about the occasional odd quirks we develop in our church bodies – because we know God uses the church in spite of its many fallible members, ourselves included. Jesus made a true and powerful statement to Peter when He said, 'the gates of hell will not prevail against it.'

We are reminded once again in these verses that God's ways are not our ways. Our wisdom is often shallow or incomplete. Sometimes, it is corrupted by our own selfish desires. Ephesians 3:10 tells us that God's wisdom is manifold. Literally, His wisdom has "many folds." He sees things from all angles and sides, past, present and future, and His wisdom is based on His perspective. It is an amazing thing that God has determined to use the church as the avenue He uses to show the principalities and powers of Satan's army just how wise He is. This is His eternal purpose for the church, which He accomplished in Jesus! Our members may not be perfect, but God's plan to use your church is not only perfect, but eternal. What part will you play in fulfilling this purpose?

Daily Journal – Day 34

Do you pray daily for your staff and leadership and fellow members in your church? Are your ministry goals well-defined and taken seriously? Is there something more, or more faithfully, you should be doing? Perhaps you are spread too thin, and you need to spend some time redefining what God's true calling is for you in your church. List the ministries you take part in within your church, and pray about your level of commitment. Then, commit to pray daily for your church that God has appointed for His eternal purpose:

_____
_____
_____
_____
_____
_____
_____
_____
_____
_____
_____
_____
_____
_____
_____

Day 35
Pure Purpose

*1 Timothy 1:5-6 ...now the purpose of the commandment is
love from a pure heart, from a good conscience,
and from sincere faith...*

Our youngest son, God bless him, was once the scourge of the church nursery. One morning when he was just under three years old, we went to collect him after the church service. He was usually the last to be picked up, and we knew it was not a good sign that the exasperated nursery workers were waiting for us at the door of the children's building. Before we could even ask, one of the workers related to us that our son had been playing with a certain little boy who had a truck that Nathan wanted to play with. After repeated requests, the little boy ignored him and refused to hand over the truck. Finally Nathan, who was built like a mini-tank, grabbed the truck, hit the boy over the head and yelled, "The Bible says to share!!"

We were hard pressed not to laugh as we disciplined him, but we managed somehow to take turns leaving the room to chuckle while the present parent explained to him how important it is not to use the Bible or our church for our own selfish purposes. In the first chapter of I Timothy, Paul recognizes that Timothy's church in Ephesus is full of people with their own agenda. They were creating strife rather than loving one another with a pure heart, a good conscience and a sincere faith. It is these things that "the Bible says to share!!"

Daily Journal – Day 35

How is your conscience? Have you spent time lately really giving it a good cleaning? Get alone with a blank sheet of paper (we needed two) and a pen. Then, list your sins. List every one of them, no matter how large or small, no matter how embarrassing or disgusting. When you cannot think of any more, pray and ask God to forgive you for those things. If more sins come to mind as you pray, write those down when you are finished, and then pray again. Repeat this process until you cannot think of anything else to add. Then, destroy the paper utterly. Shred it, burn it, or rip it into tiny pieces and throw it away, the way God does with all our sins. When you are finished, write a few words below about how this exercise made you feel:

_____
_____
_____
_____
_____
_____
_____
_____
_____
_____
_____
_____
_____
_____

Day 36
This Present Purpose

Jeremiah 29:11 ...for I know the thoughts that I think toward you, says the LORD, thoughts of peace and not of evil, to give you a future and a hope.

As fragile humans who are limited to this thing God created for us called *time*, it is very easy for us to live in the present. We become focused on how we feel, on what we have, and on how life is going for us *right now*. When things are going our way, we are quick to thank God, but when life circumstances seem to turn against us, we are very quick to take that moment to question God's love.

As a parent, there are few things more difficult than causing or allowing our children to experience momentary pain in order to give them hope for the future. Immunizations are a good example. We took our boys to get their shots when they were little and had to hold them in our arms as they cried and looked at us accusingly. The present pain was difficult, but we knew the greater reward of protecting them for the future. Our children did not know the thoughts we were thinking toward them, thoughts of health and safety, and not of evil, to give them a future and a hope free from the threat of polio and tetanus, and a host of other diseases. Our purpose was peace, but to them it just felt like pain.

God's present purpose in your life may feel like pain, but you can rest assured that His purpose is to give you a future and a hope!

Daily Journal – Day 36

Thinking from God's perspective is a daily challenge. Humanly, we want things to go according to a certain plan; we want to remain in our secure comfort zones. When those painful shots come to you, what can you do to better understand God's purposes toward you? Write about some of the times you have encountered pain that did not make sense from a human standpoint, and list a few ways that God's perspective could have changed how you handled it:

_____

_____

_____

_____

_____

_____

_____

_____

_____

_____

_____

_____

_____

_____

_____

_____

Day 37
Walk With Purpose

Colossians 2:6-7 As you therefore have received Christ Jesus the Lord, so walk in Him, rooted and built up in Him and established in the faith, as you have been taught, abounding in it with thanksgiving.

During one of our nightly family devotion times a few years ago, we came upon Colossians 2:6 and claimed it as our 'family verse.' At times before this, our various walks had been a bit weak in certain areas. We realized the truth that evening that we were walking in four different directions (in circles, more like) in our own feeble bodies, rather than walking IN Jesus. It became clear that our walk should be based on what we have received from Jesus and not on what we can accomplish, or had accomplished, on our own.

Just as the Colossians, we had been taught the truth. We had been rooted and built up in Him, but we were missing the "as you therefore have received" part. We must walk in faithfulness in the same way we have received the gift of salvation: wholly, hungrily, and desperately; with no hesitation and with much gratitude.

Also, Christians often walk apologetically. We move through life with our heads down, insecure and ashamed and trying not to offend. If this describes your walk, then straighten up and stride right! Be passionate about living in faithfulness in the same way you received Christ!

Daily Journal – Day 37

How did you receive Jesus Christ into your life? Were you passionate about your decision? Were you humbled and grateful? Did you receive His sacrifice completely and without reservation? If you answered 'yes' to all these questions, then you should be able to answer 'yes' to the question 'How are you walking?' If you are not walking in faith passionately, humbly, gratefully, completely and without reservation, you may need to make some adjustments in your attitude! What changes do you need to make in your journey toward faithfulness to make sure you are walking in the same way you are receiving?

_____

_____

_____

_____

_____

_____

_____

_____

_____

_____

_____

_____

_____

_____

_____

_____

_____

Day 38
Prosperous Purpose

Psalm 1:3 He shall be like a tree planted by the rivers of water, that brings forth its fruit in its season, whose leaf also shall not wither; and whatever he does shall prosper.

Genetically engineered fruit is the thing of the future. Already, scientists are figuring out how to make fruits stay fresh longer, be shaped for easier packaging, and even how to make an apple that tastes like grape candy. It is nerve-wracking to realize they are messing with the genetic makeup of something God created and said was 'good.' Altered fruits may look good, smell good, and seem to last, but there is no substitute for the real thing. No matter how advanced our farmers become at packaging our produce for the grocery stores, there will never be anything quite like plucking a fresh, untouched piece of fruit right off the tree or vine.

There are many so-called ministries today that try to package Christianity for the mass-market. They engineer faith until it looks fresh and easy and like a stepping stone to success, but beware! Matthew 7:21-23 tells us there are many who will claim to know God, and He will declare that He never knew them! These ministries may appear successful, but their fruits are often just for show.

True fruit is not valued by quantity, but quality, just as prosperity is not measured by dollar signs, but by blessings. God has planted us by the water, and by His purpose we are always in season!

Daily Journal – Day 38

How is your fruit production? Is it fresh and natural? Do you see results of your ministry efforts that are pure, sweet and strong? Sometimes we try to measure our successes by what looks good to man, and not by what is truly real and godly. What tangible things do you see as fruits of your ministry? Below, list the fruits you can see from your personal (not your church) ministry, and then use a few lines to describe the freshness of each of these fruits. If some of them are way past the freshness date, ask God how to freshen up your ministry efforts and get some new results!

_____

_____

_____

_____

_____

_____

_____

_____

_____

_____

_____

_____

_____

_____

_____

_____

Day 39
Pattern of Purpose

1 Timothy 1:16 ...however, for this reason I obtained mercy, that in me first Jesus Christ might show all longsuffering, as a pattern to those who are going to believe on Him for everlasting life.

Have you ever known someone that made you shake your head and think *wow, he/she is really trying God's patience?* Well, guess what? That someone is YOU! It is true of us all. Just as in Romans 7:15, Paul agonized that we do what we do not want to do, and do not do what we should, and sometimes we are too confused to even know the difference. Why, then, has God bothered to show us mercy? What is His grand purpose in loving our difficult selves? His purpose is to show His loving patience to a lost world!

Are you starting to see the pattern? Again and again, we fail. Again and again, God forgives. As long as we live, we are on an endless cycle of regret, repentance, and restoration. God's mercy is limitless!

It has been our prayer as we have penned our hearts into this book that you have seen God's patience at work through us. We are not perfect by any stretch of the imagination, but thank God we are forgiven! We hope that you are seeing in us *first* that Jesus is longsuffering. Then, that you recognize His patience in your own life and allow others to see the wonderful pattern through you!

Daily Journal – Day 39

Is God's patience clearly seen in your life? Too often, we wear the mask of perfection around others in such a way that we can not be used for this purpose. Sadly, so many Christians have become known as soldiers that shoot the wounded that we have stopped confessing our sins one to another the way the Scripture tells us to, especially to the lost! When we allow this, we are guilty of disobedience! Below, write out ways God has been patient with you, and then list at least three people you need to share those forgiven imperfections with this week (do not try God's patience and not follow through!):

_____

_____

_____

_____

_____

_____

_____

_____

_____

_____

_____

_____

_____

_____

_____

_____

Day 40
Pleasing Purpose

Hebrews 11:6 ...but without faith it is impossible to please Him, for he who comes to God must believe that He is, and that He is a rewarder of those who diligently seek Him.

Whew! What a journey we have been on together! We are tired, but we have arrived at the end of this book with you, and we are very pleased to have gotten it finished. Many of our devotions have discussed hardships and trials, so it may seem a bit contradictory to discuss one of the purposes of our faithfulness being pleasure. Pleasure-seeking seems to be associated with the world's ambitions, and not those of a Christian. The difference comes in whom we are trying to please. Are we trying to please man with our spiritual achievements, or are we trying to please God with our simple acts of faithful obedience?

We all want to know that our life brings others pleasure and joy, but there is no greater achievement than bringing pleasure to the God of the universe; the God of unconditional love and patience and mercy and sacrifice! The way to give Him pleasure is so simple, and yet so profound: have faith. Only trust Him. Without faith, it is impossible to please God. With faith it is not only *possible* to please Him, but it is guaranteed! We were created for His pleasure! What a purpose!

Thank you for sharing this wonderful journey with us! It has been our pleasure!

Daily Journal – Day 40

Is God pleased with your faith? Is your trust in Him bringing Him joy? We pray that you are a step closer on your lifelong journey of faithfulness, and that you are stronger having had companions along the way. We have gone a long way together! Now, we want you to take a moment to look back and enjoy the view! On this last day of our journey together – but the first day of the rest of your life and ministry – look back over the past 39 journal entries and jot down a few of what you feel are the most important steps you have taken along the way:

_____

_____

_____

_____

_____

_____

_____

_____

_____

_____

_____

_____

_____

_____

_____